LA GRANGE
PUBLIC LIBRARY

10 West Cossitt Avenue
La Grange, IL 60525
lagrangelibrary.org 708.215.3200

PICTURE THIS
HUMAN
BODY

KINGFISHER

First published 2013 by Kingfisher
an imprint of Macmillan Children's Books
a division of Macmillan Publishers Limited
20 New Wharf Road, London N1 9RR
Basingstoke and Oxford
Associated companies throughout the world
www.panmacmillan.com

Author: Margaret Hynes
Illustrations: Andy Crisp
Consultant: Dr Patricia Macnair
Designer: Jack Clucas
Developed by: Simon Holland

With special thanks to Peter Winfield

ISBN 978-0-7534-3503-8

Copyright © Macmillan Children's Books 2013

1 3 5 7 9 8 6 4 2
1TR/0213/UTD/WKT/140WF

A CIP catalogue record for this book
is available from the British Library.

Printed in China

PICTURE THIS

HUMAN BODY

KINGFISHER

Contents

5

Metric measures

This book is bursting with information graphics, or pictures, that illustrate facts and figures relating to the human body. Any measurements are shown using the metric system, which describes length in metres, volume in litres and weight in kilograms. If you use feet, pints and pounds instead, you are using the imperial system. The graphics on these pages compare metric and imperial amounts, and will help you to visualize the metric units.

Speed

Km/h is a unit of speed, expressing the number of kilometres travelled in one hour. This speedometer shows how km/h compare with miles per hour (mph).

- ■ km/h
- ■ mph

Volume

There are 1,000 millilitres in one litre. This is about 35 fluid ounces (35 fl oz) or just over two US pints.

Length

There are ten millimetres (10mm) in one centimetre (1cm), 100 centimetres in one metre (1m) and 1,000 metres in one kilometre (1km). This ruler shows centimetres (cm) and inches (in).

Distance

HIGHWAY 50

Newtown 1km (0.6 miles)

Townsville 10km (6 miles)

Weight

One thousand grams (1,000g) equal one kilogram (1kg) or 2.204 pounds (2.204lb). One thousand kilograms (1,000kg) equal one metric tonne (1t).

Paperclip

Coconut

Small car

1g
(0.035oz)

1kg
(2.204lb)

1 metric tonne
(1.1023113 imperial ton)

Temperature

Celsius
(metric)

Fahrenheit
(imperial)

1.52m

2.74m

1 square
metre

Area

This is calculated by multiplying the length of an area by its width. Here you can see what one square metre looks like when compared with the area of a table tennis table.

Building blocks

You are built from billions of microscopic living structures called cells. There are more than 200 different types of human cells, each of which perform different tasks. For example, sperm cells and egg cells fuse together to make babies, red blood cells carry oxygen around your body, and skin cells make up your outer layer. Cells of the same type may be organized together into tissue. Many tissues combine to form an organ, such as the stomach. Several organs work together in an organ system.

Sperm cell: 0.06mm x 0.0005mm

Red blood cell: 0.008mm

Skin cell: 0.03mm

Human egg: 0.13mm

Grain of salt

| 0mm | 0.1cm | 0.2cm | 0.3cm | 0.4cm | 0.5cm |

Microscopic living things
To get an idea of the size of cells, here are some compared with a grain of salt.

Body building

Cell

Tissue

Organ (stomach)

Organ system (digestive)

Organism (human man)

Cell components

The nucleus is a cell's control centre. Organelles, which float in a thick liquid called cytoplasm, have specific jobs to do.

Nucleus:
10% of the cell

Cytoplasm:
50% of the cell

Organelles and cell wall: 40% of the cell

Lifespan of cells

Like all living things, cells die, though some live longer than others.

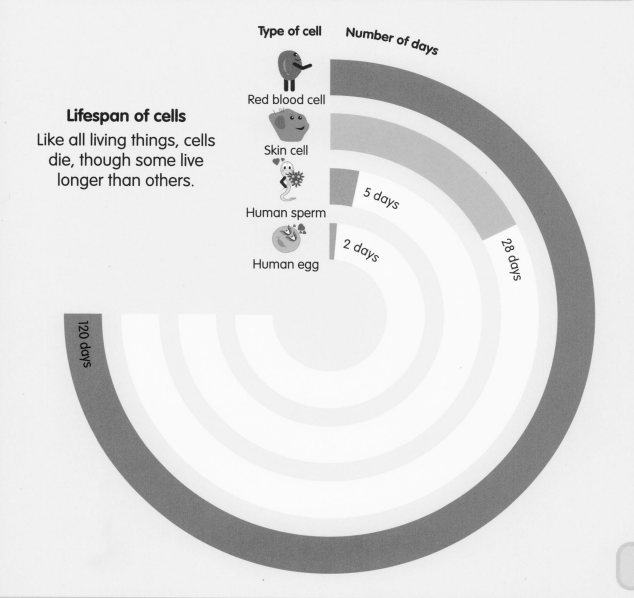

Type of cell

Number of days

Red blood cell

Skin cell

Human sperm

Human egg

5 days

2 days

28 days

120 days

Saliva per day

2% electrolytes, mucus, antibacterial compounds and enzymes........

Saliva injector

1.5L

1.0L

98% water.........

0.5L

Gastric juices per day

0.5% salt, hydrochloric acid and enzymes.....

1.5L

1.0L

99.5% water.........

0.5L

Gullet
Food chute

Stomach
Acid bath and mechanical pummel

Tongue
Taster and conveyor

`13:00:00`

Food approaching the mouth...

Mouth machine
Mechanical and chemical digester

`13:01:00`

In mouth:
up to 1 minute

1 million glands.........

`13:01:05`

In gullet:
5–10 seconds

`16:01:05`

In stomach:
3 hours

Food processing

Food is broken down into nutrients and waste as it works its way through a processing system known as the digestive system. The food is broken down mechanically by the teeth, which mash it into smaller bits, and muscles in the stomach, which pummel it into a thick soup. Chemicals made by glands in the mouth, stomach, pancreas, liver and small intestine break down the food even more so that it can be absorbed into the bloodstream and carried to the cells in the body.

Mouth: 10cm

Gullet: 25cm

Liver

Pancreas

Stomach

Small intestine: 600cm

Large intestine: 150cm

Rectum: 20cm

Tooth attachments: choppers and crushers

Incisor attachment for cutting and snipping

Canine attachment for spearing and slicing

Premolar attachment for crushing and chewing

Molar attachment for crushing and chewing

Pancreatic juices per day

1.5% enzymes and bicarbonate

1.5L
1.0L
0.5L

98.5% water

Liver bile per day

1% inorganic salts
1% cholesterol and lecithin
8% bile salt and pigment

1.5L
1.0L
0.5L

90% water

Intestinal juices per day

1.5% enzymes, mucus and inorganic solids

1.5L
1.0L
0.5L

98.5% water

20:01:05

In small intestine: 4–8 hrs

Small intestine pipeline
Nutrients and water drain from the small intestine

Large intestine duct

08:01:05 In large intestine: 12–36 hrs

Water drains from the large intestine

Blood system

Kidneys

Daily amount of excreted waste

0.25L poo

1.5L urine

Any leftover waste matter is expelled

11

Fuelling the body

Food is the body's fuel. Parts of this fuel, called nutrients, help the body to grow and repair itself, and provide the energy the body needs to power its activities. The amount of fuel your body needs depends on what you do. For example, if you stayed in bed all day, your body would need very little energy. Scientists usually measure the energy we get from food in units called calories.

Which nutrients are in the food that you eat?

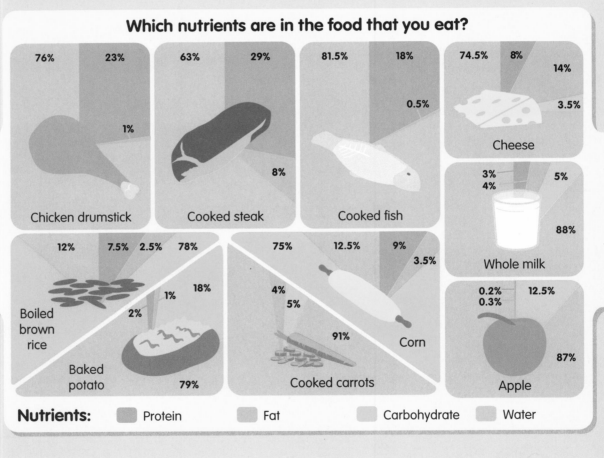

Chicken drumstick: 76% 23% 1%

Cooked steak: 63% 29% 8%

Cooked fish: 81.5% 18% 0.5%

Cheese: 74.5% 8% 14% 3.5%

Whole milk: 3% 4% 5% 88%

Boiled brown rice: 12% 7.5% 2.5% 78%

Baked potato: 1% 2% 18% 79%

Cooked carrots: 75% 12.5% 9% 3.5% 4% 5% 91%

Corn

Apple: 0.2% 0.3% 12.5% 87%

Nutrients: Protein   Fat   Carbohydrate   Water

Apple   Slice of bread   Chicken drumstick

Start   1km   2km

47 calories   85 calories   116 calories

Calorie counting
The number of calories in protein, carbohydrates and fat

1 calorie

1g	1g	1g
Protein	Carbohydrates	Fat

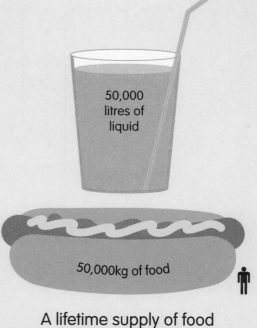

50,000 litres of liquid

50,000kg of food

A lifetime supply of food and drink for a human.

Calories burned each hour

Sleeping

75 calories

Watching TV

100 calories

Swimming

200 calories

How far will the energy in your food take you?

6km

Chocolate (32g)

Peanuts (50g)

3km 4km 5km

186 calories

295 calories

13

Lungs in action

The cells in your body use oxygen from the air around you to release the energy stored in the food you eat. A poisonous waste called carbon dioxide is produced during this process. When you breathe in, air travels through a series of tubes to tiny air bags, called alveoli, in your lungs. It is here that the oxygen is taken from the air and passed on to the cells around your body, and carbon dioxide moves in the opposite direction to be breathed out.

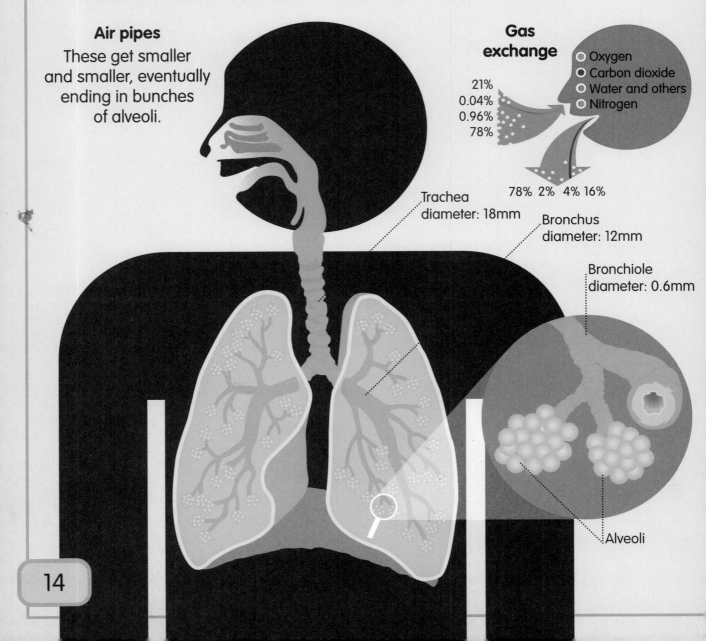

Air pipes
These get smaller and smaller, eventually ending in bunches of alveoli.

Gas exchange

○ Oxygen
○ Carbon dioxide
○ Water and others
○ Nitrogen

21%
0.04%
0.96%
78%

78% 2% 4% 16%

Trachea
diameter: 18mm

Bronchus
diameter: 12mm

Bronchiole
diameter: 0.6mm

Alveoli

If they were laid side by side, the alveoli in an adult's lung would cover an area the size of a tennis court.

Magnification x 5

1cm

10.97m

23.77m

Lung capacity

The lungs of adults are about the same size as footballs.

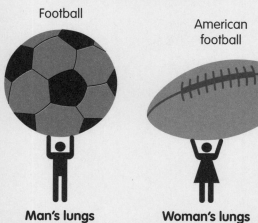

Football

American football

Man's lungs
Maximum volume: 6 litres

Woman's lungs
Maximum volume: 4.2 litres

Airflow speeds

50 60 70
40 80
30 40
30 20 50 90
20 10 60 100
70
10 110
0

■ km/h
■ mph

Normal breath   Cough   Sneeze

At rest and at play

Your breathing is deeper and slower at rest than during intense physical activity.

At rest

Heavy exercise

00:01:00

	At rest	Heavy exercise
Average volume of air breathed in one breath	0.5 litres	0.2 litres
Average volume of air breathed in one minute	6 litres	10 litres

It's in the blood!

Blood is a transport system that travels through the veins and arteries in your body, delivering oxygen and essential chemicals to where they are needed. At the same time, blood picks up toxins from around the body and carries them to the organs responsible for getting rid of waste. Blood also helps us to fight infections. More than half of our blood is made up of a clear, pale yellow liquid called plasma. Platelets, red blood cells and white blood cells float in this watery fluid, alongside chemicals such as hormones.

What is in blood?

.........90% water

............10% proteins, hormones, vitamins and cholesterol

55%............Plasma

45%............Cellular components

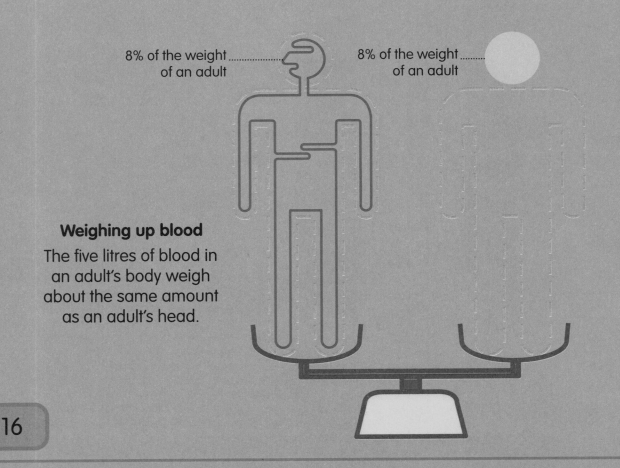

8% of the weight of an adult

8% of the weight of an adult

Weighing up blood

The five litres of blood in an adult's body weigh about the same amount as an adult's head.

Cellular components

There are 600 red blood cells for every one white blood cell and every 40 platelets in blood.

- White blood cell
- Red blood cell
- Platelet

Haemoglobin.............................33%

Blood-red cell

An iron-rich protein called haemoglobin gives red blood cells their colour.

Daily iron recycling

When red blood cells die, they release iron back into the blood system.

25mg

Oxygen transporter

One haemoglobin molecule can carry four oxygen molecules.

Transport network

The body has an efficient transport network to shuttle blood supplies to where they are needed. Every minute, about five litres of blood travel once around the body in a one-way circuit. The blood is ferried in tubes, called blood vessels, and is kept on the move by a powerful pump – the heart. This beats about once every second and more than 100,000 times a day. On its journey, blood distributes nutrients, oxygen and other substances, and collects waste and by-products.

Brain

Right lung

Left lung

Heart

Liver

Spleen

Stomach

Intestines

Right kidney

Left kidney

Brain line

Coronary line

Kidney line

Muscle line

Digestion line

Lung line

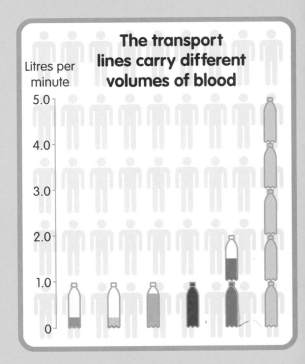

The transport lines carry different volumes of blood

Litres per minute

5.0
4.0
3.0
2.0
1.0
0

A blood cell travels about 480km in its 120-day lifetime, shown here as a trek across Switzerland.

If laid end to end, our blood vessels would stretch 150,000km, or nearly four times around the world.

A beating heart pumps huge volumes of blood as time passes by...

- 1 minute: 5 litres (1 small petrol can)

- 1 hour: 300 litres (more than 2 oil barrels)

- 1 day: 7,200 litres (almost 45 oil barrels)

A blood cell takes 60 seconds to complete one circuit of the body.

Million barrels
- 2.0
- 1.5
- 1.0
- 0.5
- 0

- 70 years: 184 million litres (1.2 million oil barrels), filling more than half the capacity of a supertanker

The skin you're in

Without skin, your body's organs and fluid parts would spill out. They would also be exposed to harmful microbes, the weather, and bumps and knocks. You would not experience the sensations of touch and temperature, and your body could overheat or freeze. Human skin has three layers. The outer one, the epidermis, is shed and replaced approximately every 35 days.

The many roles of your hard-working skin

Natural sunscreen
that protects the body from the sun's harmful ultraviolet (UV) rays

Body armour,
made up of fat, that protects the organs and bones by absorbing shock

Sensory organ
that responds to physical contact, heat, cold, vibration, pressure and pain

Temperature controller
that uses hair, blood vessels and sweat glands to keep your body at the ideal temperature of 37°C

Waterproof coat
that prevents substances getting into your body and moisture from getting out

Vitamin maker
that uses sunlight to make vitamin D

Infection fighter
that detects microbes and defends your body against them

Skin structure

Skin layers

- Hair shaft
- Sweat pore
- Epidermis
- Dermis
- Subcutaneous
- Hair follicle
- Sensory receptor
- Artery
- Vein
- Fat
- Sweat gland

Sweat soda

330ml

The sweat glands in an adult's feet can produce enough fluid in one day to fill a soda can.

Change of skin

You shed about 10.4 epidermal skin layers each year.

0											1	**years**
0	35	70	105	140	175	210	245	280	315	350	365	**days**

How long is your skin safe from sun damage in different levels of UV intensity?

Minutes in the sun without extra protection

0 10 20 30 40 50 60 70 80 90 100 110 120

UV intensity

- Minimal
- Low
- Moderate
- High
- Very high

Skin type and the time range in which sun damage first occurs

- Skin that always burns
- Skin that usually burns
- Skin that sometimes burns
- Skin that rarely burns

From head to toe

You may think of your hair and nails only as things to be styled and trimmed, but they actually have more practical uses. The millions of hairs all over your body insulate you against the cold, while the hard surface of your nails helps to protect the tips of your fingers and toes. Of course, your nails are also useful for scratching an itch! Hair and nails are modified forms of the top layer of your skin – they are all formed from a substance called keratin.

cm	Year
0	0
15	1
30	2
45	3
60	4
75	5
90	6

The long and short of it
Each strand of your head hair can grow up to 15cm every year, and has a lifespan of six years.

12 tonnes

100,000 strands of hair

Elephant strength
All the hair on your head combined is strong enough to support the weight of two elephants.

Hairy humans

Humans have about five million hairs growing on their body – roughly the same amount as a gorilla has!

Finger

Big toe

mm   0   10   20   30   40   50

Nail growth

Your fingernails grow about three times faster than your toenails.

One year's growth (8mm)

Grubby fingernails

About 95 per cent of the bacteria on your hands is usually found under the fingernails.

1% bacteria

Body defences

The body is designed to protect itself against infectious microbes. Your skin forms an external defensive layer. If you cut yourself, your blood forms a scab that stops microbes getting in. Most of the microbes that get into your mouth drop into your stomach acid and are killed. Hairs in your nose filter the air you breathe in. If nasty microbes get past these defences, an army of white blood cells swallows up and destroys the invaders.

Lines of defence

First line of defence

  Physical barriers

Second line of defence

  Producers and developers of white blood cells

  Concentrations of white blood cells

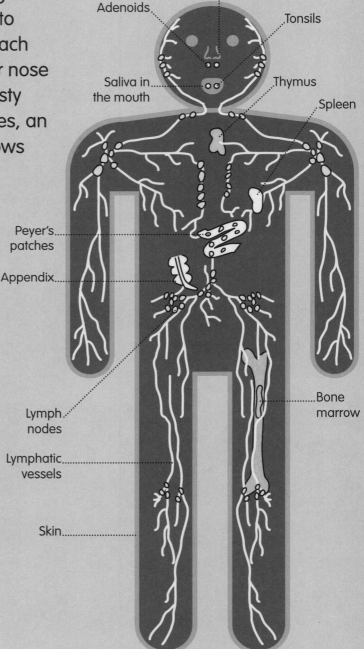

Adenoids

Hair and mucus in the nose

Tonsils

Saliva in the mouth

Thymus

Spleen

Peyer's patches

Appendix

Lymph nodes

Lymphatic vessels

Skin

Bone marrow

A timeline for wound healing

Days 0 to 2
Blood clots and scab begins to form

Day 3
Cells multiply to make new skin tissue

Weeks to months
Skin re-forms, closing the wound

This scale shows how acidic or alkaline certain fluids are. Battery acid is the most acidic of the fluids shown. Stomach acid is also a strong acid, so it would have no trouble killing infectious microbes.

White blood cells at war

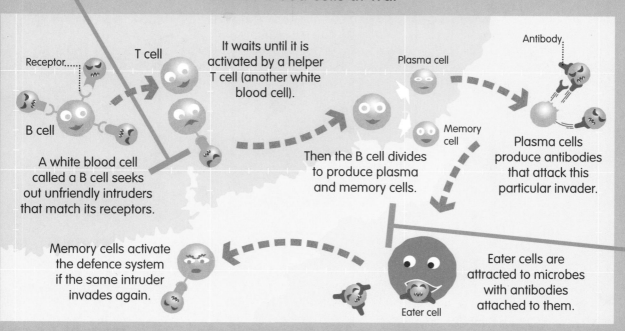

A white blood cell called a B cell seeks out unfriendly intruders that match its receptors.

It waits until it is activated by a helper T cell (another white blood cell).

Then the B cell divides to produce plasma and memory cells.

Plasma cells produce antibodies that attack this particular invader.

Eater cells are attracted to microbes with antibodies attached to them.

Memory cells activate the defence system if the same intruder invades again.

Alien invasion

Bacteria split in two every 20 minutes. If invading
bacteria were left to develop, there could be enough
to cover the entire surface of the Earth within 36 hours.

Body invaders

When unfriendly microbes, such as bacteria and viruses,
invade your body they reproduce very rapidly, damaging your
body tissues as they multiply. Your body responds to this damage
with symptoms, such as coughing, fevers, aches and tiredness.
It is these symptoms that make you feel ill. Viruses and bacterial
infections can be spread through the air or through contact with
things that have the harmful microbes on them.

Cell invaders
Three steps to a
successful viral invasion

Step 1
A single virus
takes over a cell

Step 2
The virus uses the cell to
make duplicate viruses

Step 3
Viruses burst out, destroying
the cell on the way, ready to
infect more cells

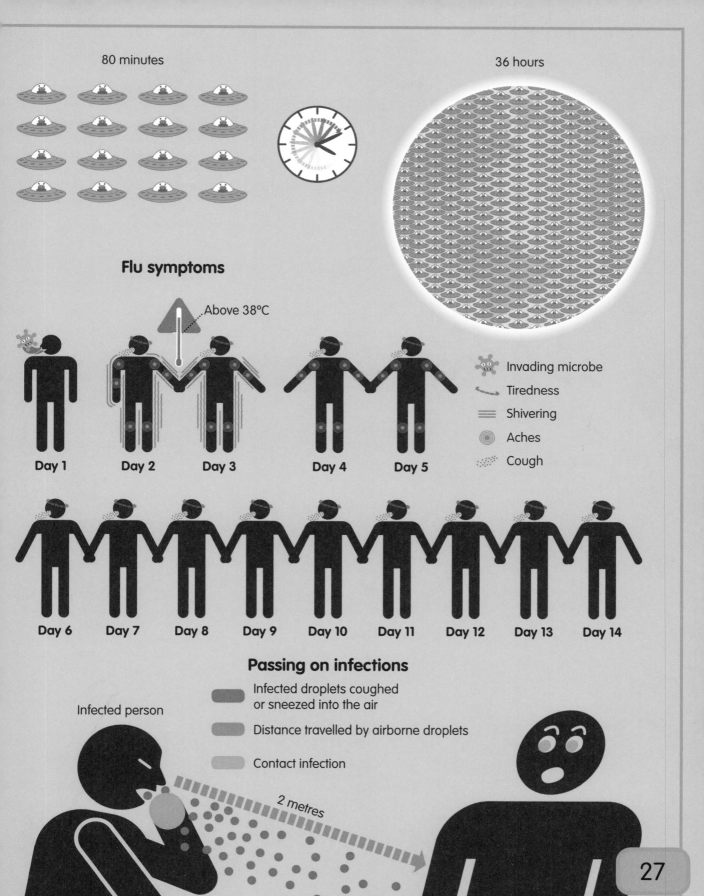

80 minutes

36 hours

Flu symptoms

Above 38°C

Day 1 **Day 2** **Day 3** **Day 4** **Day 5**

Invading microbe
Tiredness
Shivering
Aches
Cough

Day 6 **Day 7** **Day 8** **Day 9** **Day 10** **Day 11** **Day 12** **Day 13** **Day 14**

Passing on infections

Infected person

Infected droplets coughed
or sneezed into the air

Distance travelled by airborne droplets

Contact infection

2 metres

27

Water of life

More than half of your weight is made up of water. Your body needs this water to carry out essential processes. For example, water removes wastes from your vital organs, carries nutrients to your cells and regulates your body temperature. You lose water from your body when you urinate, sweat and breathe out. If you don't replace this water by drinking and eating, you become dehydrated.

Water in the body
The amount of water in your body reduces as you get older.

80%	65%	50%
Newborn baby	Average adult	Elderly person

Water in the average adult's organs, bones and teeth

Bones 22%

Blood 95%

Teeth 10%....

Skin 71%

Total in the body 40 litres

Brain 85%

Muscles 73%

Lungs 80%

Kidneys 80%

Heart 77%

Liver 73%

Water in food

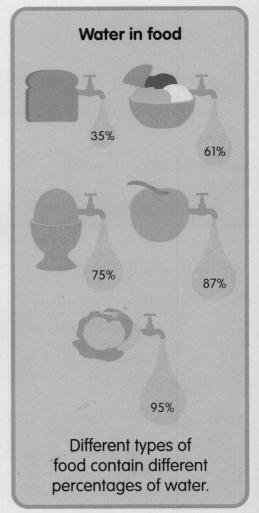

35%

61%

75%

87%

95%

Different types of food contain different percentages of water.

28

Water levels

Our body must maintain a balance between the water we take in and the water we lose.

Water taken in

12% metabolic water (produced in the body during chemical processes)

28% from food

60% from drinks

2 litres

Water lost

6% in solid waste

13% in breath

19% by diffusion and in sweat

62% in urine

2 litres

Stages of dehydration

The symptoms of dehydration become more serious the more water you lose.

1.5 litres

3 litres

4 litres

Symptoms

| Thirst | Sluggishness, extreme tiredness, nausea and emotional instability | Clumsiness, headaches, plus increased body temperature, pulse rate and breathing rate |

5 litres

6 litres

9 litres

12 litres

| Dizziness, slurred speech, weakness and confusion | Delirium, swollen tongue, circulatory problems, decreased blood volume and kidney failure | Inability to swallow, painful urination and cracked skin | Life-threatening level of dehydration |

Waste disposal

Your body creates a variety of wastes while it carries out essential chemical processes. Most of these wastes are filtered from your blood by two organs called kidneys. The kidneys return useful substances to the body system. They also send excess water and waste in the form of urine (wee) down tubes to a bag-like organ known as the bladder. When this is full, your brain tells you to release the urine by going to the toilet.

The volume of blood that the heart pumps to the kidneys each day would fill a small dumpster.

1,080 litres

Urine sample

A healthy person's urine contains these substances (right), roughly in the amounts shown.

95% water

1.5 litres

5% waste substances

A day's urine output

Waste substances

Uric acid: 0.6g

Bicarbonate ions: 1.2g
Creatinine: 2.7g

Potassium ions: 3.2g

Sodium ions: 4.1g

Chloride ions: 6.6g

Urea: 25.5g

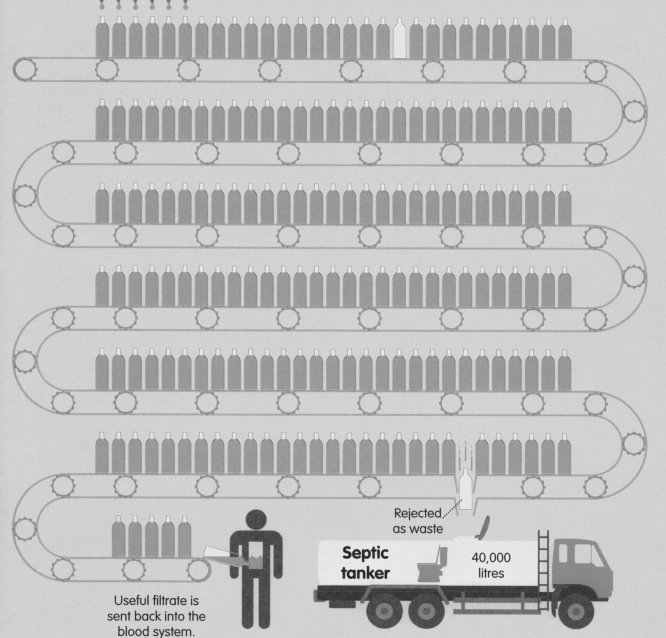

Blood pumped from the heart

Blood sent back into the blood system

Blood filtration system

Filtrate, made up of water and dissolved substances

Filtration and disposal

The filtration system removes 180 litres of fluid from the blood. Of this amount, 1.5 litres are urine, which is expelled as waste.

Rejected as waste

Septic tanker

40,000 litres

Useful filtrate is sent back into the blood system.

1 litre of filtrate

1 litre of urine

In a lifetime, the average human produces enough urine to fill a septic tanker.

Coping with extremes

Our bodies have heat regulation systems that help us to stay at an optimum (ideal) temperature of 37°C in both warm and cold conditions. But our bodies can't cope with extremes of cold and heat, or low oxygen levels. We have learned to overcome these conditions by adopting survival strategies, such as wearing warm clothing, running air conditioning and using an air supply.

37°C   25°C

Cold water survival time

Hours in the water

Slim chance of survival

Strong possibility of survival if rescued

6

5

4

3

2

1

0°C   5°C   10°C   15°C

Water temperature

Temperature control

When it gets cold, the body diverts heat to the core organs.

Headaches and dizziness

No symptoms

Hazards of a decreasing core temperature

The stages of hypothermia

37°C to 35°C
Shivering

Death is likely

Everest
8,848m

Organs begin
to shut down

Hallucinations

Percentage of
oxygen available

Height above sea level

These pictures show the
symptoms suffered by a
person who is unused to
high altitudes, and who
is climbing without
an air supply.

Can't remember what you
are supposed to be doing

Aconcagua
6,962m

Inability to work out
what is around you

Kilimanjaro
5,895m

Mont Blanc
4,808m

Inability to control the
movement of the hands

Ben
Nevis
1,344m

35°C to 33°C
Nausea and
disorientation

32°C to 28°C
Unconsciousness

9,000m
33%
8,000m
37%
7,500m
40%
6,000m
49%
5,000m
55%
3,500m
66%
2,500m
75%
1,000m
89%

Mind control

The brain is the body's control centre. It operates all necessary functions of the body, such as regulating your heartbeat and breathing, sending you to sleep and telling your body how to move. But the brain also receives and interprets information from the outside world, allows you to think, stores your memories, gives you personality and controls your emotions. The brain governs all these things by sending and receiving millions of tiny electrical signals through a network of billions of nerve cells, called neurons.

Brain power
The brain uses 23 watts of energy, which is enough to power a light bulb.

Side view of the right-hand part of the brain

Sensation

Motion

Thinking

Speech

Hearing

Vision

Feelings and emotions

Cerebrum 85%

Balance

Cerebellum 11%

Eye and face movement

Brain areas
There are three main parts of the brain. Areas within these parts are responsible for different functions.

Breathing and heart rate

Brainstem 4%

Thoughtful brain

You think 70,000 thoughts a day.

Oxygen use

Your brain uses about 20 per cent of the oxygen you inhale (take in).

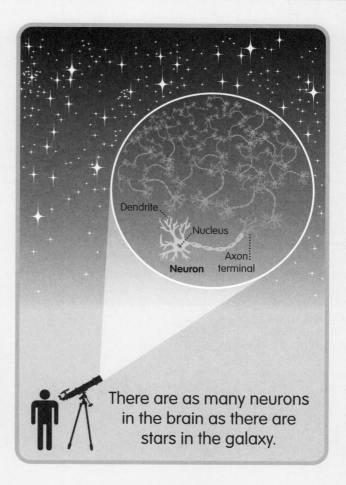

Dendrite

Nucleus

Neuron

Axon terminal

There are as many neurons in the brain as there are stars in the galaxy.

A brain of two halves

The left half of the brain is its logical side. The right half is the creative side.

Brain size

The average brain is the size of a cantaloupe (a small melon) and weighs about 1.4kg.

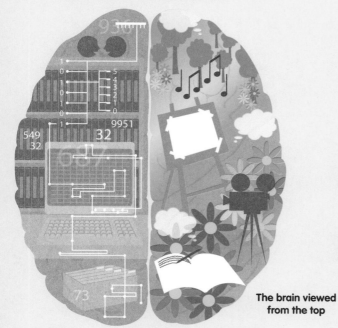

The brain viewed from the top

35

The body's Internet

Your body has built-in wiring and communications in the form of the nervous system. This coordinates and controls almost all your body's activities. It works much like the system that we use to make telephone calls and surf the Internet. Both are designed to send messages from one place to another. The messages travel in the form of electrical signals or pulses, along bundles of wire-like structures. The body's wires are called nerves.

The nervous system has three main parts: the brain, the spinal cord extending down the back and the peripheral nerves throughout the body.

Peripheral nervous system

A network of nerves that branch out from the brain and spinal cord to every part of the body.

Central nervous system

This consists of the brain and spinal cord, which links the brain to many parts of the body.

Touch

Limb movement

Hearing

Eye movement

Releasing urine from the bladder

Somatic nervous system

Some of the messages are about sensations, and others are about movements that we make at will and control with our thoughts.

Message speeds

Message to
Muscle

Brain

119 metres per second

76.2 metres per second

Message from
Brain

Touch

Distance travelled in 1 second

0.61 metres per second

Pain

Brain

Sympathetic

Dilates pupils

Accelerates heartbeat

Constricts bronchi

Inhibits bladder contraction

Parasympathetic

Constricts pupils

Slows down heartbeat

Dilates bronchi

Contracts bladder

Autonomic nervous system

This deals with automatic body processes. These happen on their own without our awareness.

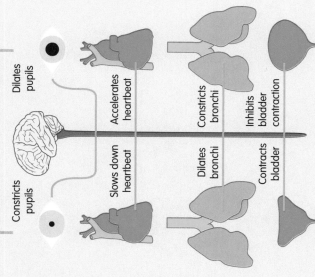

Sensory receptors

Muscle

Sensory neuron

Motor neuron

Spinal cord

Reflex action

The spinal cord controls automatic and rapid actions called reflexes. These include snatching your hand away from the heat of a flame.

A good night's sleep
Four stages of deep NREM sleep are
followed by lighter REM sleep, during which
the eyes move back and forth rapidly.

Midnight | 1am | 2am | 3am | 4am | 5am | 6am | 7am | 8am

Sleepy heads

It may seem like we do nothing
when we sleep, however
the brain is actually very active
during this time. Scientists use
an EEG machine to detect and
display brainwaves – the patterns
of electrical activity produced by
the brain cells. The EEG pattern
changes in a predictable way
several times during a single
period of sleep. There are two
basic forms of sleep: rapid eye
movement (REM) sleep and
non-rapid REM (NREM) sleep.

State of consciousness	Seconds
	0 5 10 15 20
Awake	
NREM sleep Stage 1	
NREM sleep Stage 2	
NREM sleep Stage 3	
NREM sleep Stage 4	
REM sleep	

Brainwave activity
There are fewer brainwaves during
NREM sleep than REM sleep.

38

Sweet dreams

An adult has about five dreams in one night, usually during REM sleep.

Hours of sleep in a 24-hour period

| | 1 | 2 | 3 | 4 | 5 | 6 | 7 | 8 | 9 | 10 | 11 | 12 | 13 | 14 | 15 | 16 |

Age of sleeping person

Infants
(1–15 days)

Toddlers
(2–3 years)

Child
(10–13 years)

Adults
(19–30 years)

Elderly person
(70–85 years)

■ NREM sleep

□ REM sleep

Work, rest and play

On average, people spend about one-third of the year asleep.

? 56 102 2,487... ? 34... 2... ?

33%
....................122 days

67%
243 days..................

Sight

Your eyes take pictures of the world around you, then send them to your brain for processing. A lens in your eye acts like a camera lens, focussing light rays onto the inside lining of the back wall of the eye, called the retina. Here, special cells record the pattern created by the rays and send the information to the brain. The brain then works out what your eyes are seeing.

Cross-section of a human eye

Cones handle colour vision and detail

Rods detect black and white, and handle vision in low light

Retina

Parts of the eye

Eyelid protects the eye

Pupil lets in light

Cornea directs light rays through the pupil

Lens focuses light onto the retina

Optic nerve carries information to the brain

Light-detecting cells	Surface coverage
Rods	94.5%
Green cones	3.5%
Red cones	1.75%
Blue cones	0.25%

Hearing

As with your sight, your hearing gives your brain information about what is happening around you. The sounds that you hear, such as people talking, are created by invisible vibrations called sound waves. These travel through the air in all directions. Your ears collect the sound waves, and first turn them into mechanical vibrations, then electrical signals that your brain can understand.

Light, lens, action

Micro-processor

Objects reflect light

Light rays

Lens

The retina and camera microchip record an upside-down image.

Image processors

How the processed images appear

Brain

Hear and how

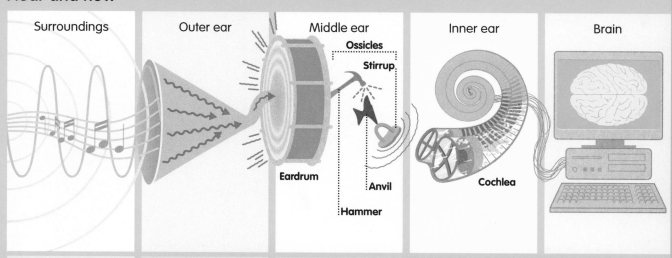

Surroundings	Outer ear	Middle ear	Inner ear	Brain

Ossicles

Stirrup

Eardrum

Anvil

Hammer

Cochlea

Reception
Invisible sound waves move through the air and approach your ears.

Collection
Your trumpet-shaped outer ear collects sound waves and directs them towards your eardrum.

Vibration
The waves strike the eardrum, causing it and the tiny ossicle bones to vibrate and create pressure waves.

Electrical notes
Fluid in the inner ear is forced over structures that, a bit like keyboard keys, convert the pressure into electrical signals.

Processing
Electrical signals are sent to the brain, where they are processed so that you hear sound.

41

Smell and taste

▲ 20% intensity   ▲ 100% intensity

Our senses of smell and taste work in similar ways. Groups of olfactory cells in the nose detect floating molecules of scent in the air, called odorants. The nose can distinguish more than 10,000 different scents. Taste buds in the mouth detect flavourants, but our mouths pick up only five basic flavours. As we eat, the brain receives information from both senses. It comes to associate the odours with the flavours, creating an overall 'taste sensation'.

Familiar scent
The odour of perfume is only one-fifth as powerful to a person who usually wears it than it is to other people.

Reception area
The 12 million olfactory receptor cells in your nose cover an area about the size of a rose petal.

Olfactory receptor cells

Odorant molecule

10 square cm

Where are the 10,000 taste buds in your mouth located?

90% on the tongue

10% in the rest of the mouth

Five basic flavours

Our taste buds register differing proportions of these flavours in different foods and drinks.

Sweet

Sour

Salty

Bitter

Umami

Taste sensation

Without our sense of smell, our food would be about 80 per cent less flavoursome.

Without smell
20% intensity

With smell
100% intensity

Sensory part
of the right half
of the brain

Sensory body map
The most sensitive areas of the body have the highest density of sensors, which are connected to the largest sensory processing areas in the brain.

Above: here are the relative amounts of brain area that process sensory information from the parts of the body shown in the same colours on the right.

Right: this shows what a human body would look like if each part grew in proportion to the area of the brain concerned with its sensory perception. The larger areas in this picture are the most sensitive.

Touch

Millions of sensors in your skin allow you to feel a range of sensations, from the pain of touching a hot flame to the tickling of a feather as it brushes against your skin. The receptors send messages along nerves to the spinal cord and the sensory part of the brain, where the information is processed.

Hotspots

Your head and hands have the greatest concentration of heat sensors in your body.

Thick and thin skin

Sensors in the thin skin on your forehead can detect the weight of a 2-milligram fruit fly, but you wouldn't sense it on the thick skin of your fingertip.

Sensory thermometer

Here are the temperatures at which you detect the sensations of heat, cold, pain and numbness.

Pain

45°C

40°C

Hot receptors perceive hot sensations

35°C

30°C

25°C

20°C

Cold receptors perceive cold sensations

15°C

10°C

5°C

Numbness

Moving about

The human body is a mechanical masterpiece capable of performing a huge range of movements. Without its framework of bones, called the skeleton, and the skeletal muscles that cover it, your body would be a motionless blob on the ground. Joints between the bones make your skeleton flexible. Under the control of your brain, your muscles contract or relax to move your bones at the joints, allowing you to run, jump and perform many other movements.

Where bones meet

The type of joint that connects two bones determines how those bones move in relation to each other.

Pivot joints (neck and forearm) allow one bone to rotate around another.

Ball and socket joints (shoulders and hips) permit movement in almost every direction.

Hinge joints (elbow and knee) enable movement much like the opening and closing of a hinged door.

Saddle joints (thumbs) allow movement back and forth and from side to side.

Plane joints (wrists and ankles) allow sliding or gliding movements.

Ellipsoid joints (fingers) allow movement back and forth, side to side, and a very small amount of rotation.

Your main muscle groups

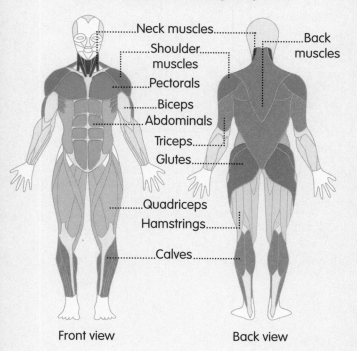

Neck muscles
Shoulder muscles
Pectorals
Biceps
Abdominals
Triceps
Glutes
Quadriceps
Hamstrings
Calves
Back muscles

Front view

Back view

Pedal power

Here are the leg muscles you use when you pedal your bike.

Biceps contract
Triceps relax
Biceps relax
Triceps contract

Muscle mechanics

Many of our muscle groups work in pairs. While one group contracts (shortens), the other group relaxes. This makes the bones move.

- Glutes
- Quadriceps
- Hamstrings
- Calves
- Hip flexor (quadriceps)

The coloured lines (left) show at which point each set of muscles is used during the operation of the bike's pedals.

New life

There are around seven billion people in the world, and they all began in the same way. The male reproductive system makes cells, called sperm, that fertilize, or fuse with, a female egg cell to make a fertilized egg. This forms an embryo that divides repeatedly, producing a foetus after about eight weeks. This grows inside the mother's uterus and develops into a baby.

Sperm slide: 30cm

Assault course
The male releases about 250 million sperm into the female. The sperms' journey to the egg is so tough that only one of them will make it.

Sperm and egg size
If you were a sperm, the egg would be the size of a ten-storey building.

250 million sperm

Deadly acid pool
The sperm have to endure a 10cm-long swim through acidic fluids in the vagina.

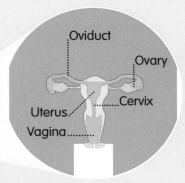

Penis..........
Urethra.....................Testis

Oviduct
Ovary
Uterus...
Cervix
Vagina..........

Male reproductive system
Sperm are produced in the two testes.
They are released through the urethra,
which is a tube inside the penis.

Female reproductive system
Each month, one of the ovaries produces
a ripe egg cell. This makes its way along
the oviduct, towards the uterus.

Day 1:
fertilization

Day 2:
cell divides

Day 3:
cells compact

Day 4: different
types of cells form

Day 5:
cavity forms

Day 6:
implantation

About 60,000
sperm survive
the 2-cm-high
climb to reach
the cervix.

Embryo growth
After fertilization, the egg cell
splits into several cells and
eventually implants itself into
the wall of the uterus.

Sperm meets egg
One out of 15 to 24 sperm
cells fertilizes the egg.

..........10%
survive
90% die

Maze-like cervix
Only 3,000 sperm
make it out of
the cervix alive.

The gauntlet
About 50 sperm
survive the attacks
of white blood
cells in the uterus.

Lazy river
The 10-cm-long
oviducts are paradise
for the sperm.

Growing and developing

It takes more than 20 years for the human body to grow and develop fully. During this time, you lose a set of teeth and replace it with another set. Your body proportions change and you become stronger, so you can do more and more physical things. Your brain also develops, gradually turning you into an independent person capable of making your own decisions – an adult!

Week 1
Dot on this 'i'

Week 4
Poppy seed

Week 8
Raspberry

Week 12
Plum

Week 16
Avocado

Week 20
Banana

Week 24
Cantaloupe melon

Week 28
Aubergine

Becoming mature

One of the last parts of the brain to mature is the area that controls your ability to make sensible decisions and plan out things.

Age 5

Age 8

Age 12

Area that makes you mature

Age 16

Age 20

☐ Less mature
■ Mature

Teething times

Your baby teeth and permanent teeth appear in the order shown here.

Baby teeth

Age
☐ 6–10 months
☐ 8–13 months
☐ 10–16 months
☐ 13–19 months
☐ 16–23 months
☐ 23–33 months

Permanent teeth

Age
☐ 6–8 years
☐ 7–9 years
☐ 9–12 years
☐ 11–13 years
☐ 17–21 years

Week 32
Ambercup squash

Week 36
Honeydew melon

Week 40
Watermelon

Fruit of the womb

During the nine months that it is in the womb (uterus), a baby grows from being the size of the dot on this "i" to the size of a watermelon.

Body proportions

The proportions of the head and arms are very different in babies and adults.

Baby   Age 20

Baby

Age 20

Standing tall

From about five years old, growth gradually slows down. Then from about 10 to 13 years in girls, and 13 to 15 years in boys, growth speeds up again.

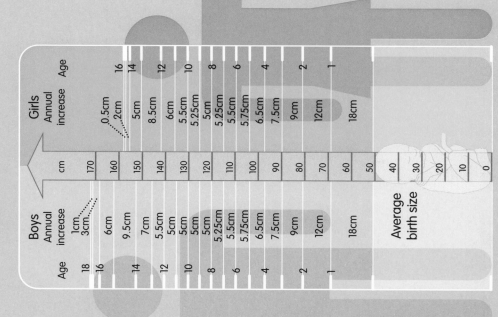

Boys Annual increase	Age	cm	Girls Annual increase	Age
1cm	18		0.5cm	16
3cm	16	170	2cm	14
		160		
6cm	14	150	5cm	12
9.5cm		140	8.5cm	
7cm	12	130	6cm	10
5.5cm			5.5cm	
5cm	10	120	5.25cm	
5cm			5cm	8
5cm	8	110	5.25cm	
5.25cm		100	5.5cm	6
5.5cm	6		5.75cm	
5.75cm		90	6.5cm	4
6.5cm	4		7.5cm	
7.5cm		80	9cm	2
9cm	2	70	12cm	
12cm		60		1
18cm	1	50	18cm	
		40		
Average birth size		30		
		20		
		10		
		0		

Code for life

Every cell in your body contains a set of coded instructions that tell the cell what it should be doing, and how to do it. The instructions are written in an alphabet that is only four letters long – A, T, C and G – and they come in the form of a molecule called deoxyribonucleic acid (DNA). This has a twisted ladder shape, known as a double helix. The letters of the DNA alphabet are substances called bases. These make up the 'ladder rungs'. Sugars and other atoms form the 'handrail'.

23 pairs of chromosomes in the cell nucleus

Human cell

Chromosomes are made from long DNA molecules

DNA double helix

Unlocking the codes

Base pairs can come in any order down the chain

Bases

A (adenine)   T (thymine)

C (cytosine)   G (guanine)

A joins with T only, and G joins with C only.

Writing the code

It would take a typist working 8-hour days 50 years to type the entire human code, which covers about 750,000 A4 pages.

Height of the stacks of paper

7.5m
7m
6.5m
6m
5.5m
5m
4.5m
4m
3.5m
3m
2.5m
2m
1.5m
1m
0.5m
0m

5 10 15 20 25   Years   30 35 40 45 50

Sharing DNA

■ 99% shared DNA   ■ 1% different DNA

Many scientists believe most of our DNA is the same as that of a chimpanzee.

How long is your DNA?
If it were laid end to end, all the DNA in your body would span the diameter of the Solar System twice.

Cracking the code
The purpose of about 95 per cent of our DNA has yet to be worked out by scientists.

Archives

Research laboratory

5%   95%

It's in the genes!

Segments of DNA called genes determine which physical features we inherit from our parents. Genes carry the codes for making proteins in the cell. Proteins build everything in your body: bones, teeth, hair, muscles and more. Each parent passes on a copy of their genes to their children. Certain inherited traits dominate over others. For example, if one parent has freckles yet the other parent doesn't, their offspring will have freckles, as this is a dominant trait.

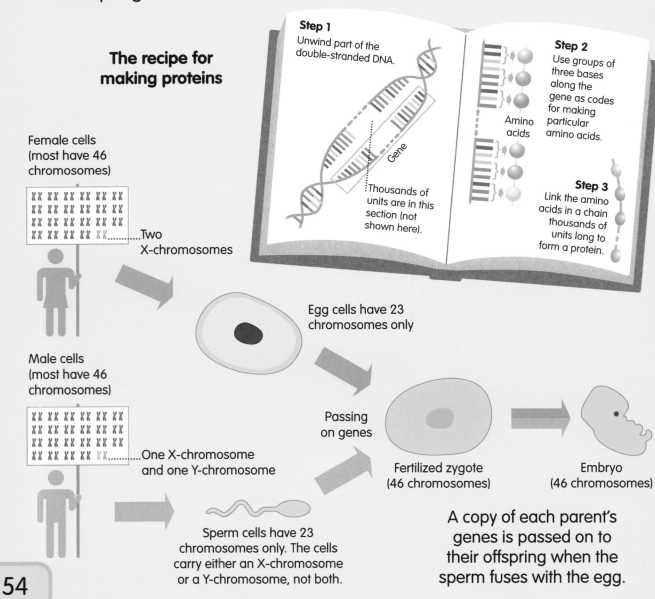

The recipe for making proteins

Step 1
Unwind part of the double-stranded DNA.

Gene

Thousands of units are in this section (not shown here).

Step 2
Use groups of three bases along the gene as codes for making particular amino acids.

Amino acids

Step 3
Link the amino acids in a chain thousands of units long to form a protein.

Female cells (most have 46 chromosomes)

Two X-chromosomes

Male cells (most have 46 chromosomes)

One X-chromosome and one Y-chromosome

Egg cells have 23 chromosomes only

Sperm cells have 23 chromosomes only. The cells carry either an X-chromosome or a Y-chromosome, not both.

Passing on genes

Fertilized zygote (46 chromosomes)

Embryo (46 chromosomes)

A copy of each parent's genes is passed on to their offspring when the sperm fuses with the egg.

54

Boy or girl?

The sex of offspring is determined by whether or not the egg is fertilized by an X-carrying sperm or a Y-carrying sperm.

Parent 1	Parent 2	Probability
●	+ ●	= Brown 75% / Green 19% / Blue 6%
●	+ ●	= Brown 50% / Green 0% / Blue 50%
●	+ ●	= Brown 50% / Green 38% / Blue 12%
●	+ ●	= Brown 0% / Green 1% / Blue 99%
●	+ ●	= Brown 0% / Green 50% / Blue 50%
●	+ ●	= Brown 0% / Green 75% / Blue 25%

You've got your parents'...

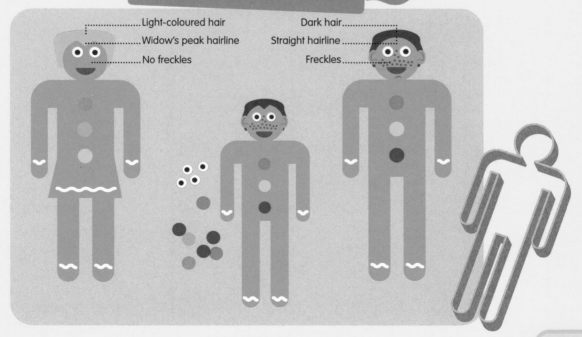

Light-coloured hair .... Dark hair
Widow's peak hairline .... Straight hairline
No freckles .... Freckles

This gingerbread kid has inherited the dominant traits from each of its parents. Can you spot which ones they are?

55

Keeping healthy

The best way to keep your body in tip-top condition is to take care of it. Destroy as many harmful microbes as possible before they get into your body by washing your hands regularly. Stay fit by exercising. This will also help you to keep your body weight at the right level, in combination with eating a balanced diet. Always be aware of the harmful effects of the sun and protect your hearing in noisy places.

Usually washed

Missed frequently

Missed most frequently

Top of hand   Underside of hand

Wash your hands well

People frequently miss certain areas of the hands while washing them. Do you clean the areas missed by others?

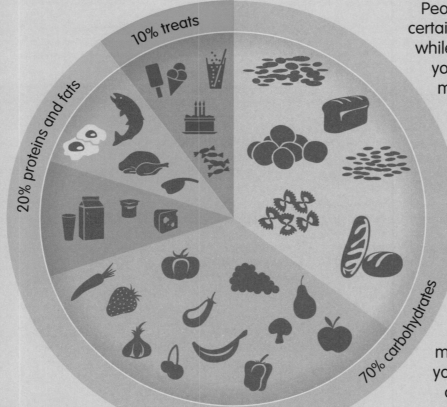

10% treats

20% proteins and fats

70% carbohydrates

Balanced diet

The sizes of these segments show how much of each type of food you should eat to maintain a balanced diet. Such a diet must contain a wide range of foods.

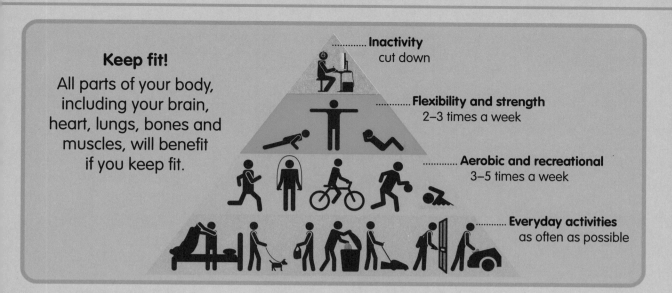

Keep fit!

All parts of your body, including your brain, heart, lungs, bones and muscles, will benefit if you keep fit.

.... **Inactivity**
cut down

.... **Flexibility and strength**
2–3 times a week

.... **Aerobic and recreational**
3–5 times a week

.... **Everyday activities**
as often as possible

Volume control

Know how loud the sounds around you are, and be aware of the maximum time that your hearing can put up with those volumes.

Raindrops
Normal conversation
Noisy party
Hairdryer
Whispering
Pneumatic drill
Jet aircraft
Pain threshold

60 80
40 100
20 120
0 **Decibels** 140

Decibels	Maximum exposure time
115	15 minutes
110	30 minutes
105	1 hour
102	1.5 hours
100	2 hours
97	3 hours
95	4 hours
92	6 hours
90	8 hours

Protect your skin from harmful ultraviolet (UV) rays

UV intensity of the sun

Low | Medium | High | Very high | Extremely high

Protection required

- 🧴 Sunscreen
- 👓 Sunglasses
- 👒 Hat
- 👕 Long-sleeved top
- ⛱ Stay in the shade
- 🕐 Avoid the sun between 10am and 4pm
- 🚪 Stay indoors

Useful charts

Recommended daily amount of calories

Age	Male	Female
0 to 3 months	545	515
4 to 6 months	690	645
7 to 9 months	825	765
10 to 12 months	920	865
1 to 3 years	1,230	1,165
4 to 6 years	1,715	1,545
7 to 10 years	1,970	1,740
11 to 14 years	2,220	1,845
15 to 18 years	2,755	2,110
19 to 50 years	2,550	1,940
51 to 59 years	2,550	1,900
60 to 64 years	2,380	1,900
65 to 74 years	2,330	1,900
75+ years	2,100	1,810

Blood types

Blood types are identified by the presence, or absence, of chemical markers: A or B agglutinogen. The types can also be RhD positive or negative, so your blood can be one of eight types.

Marker on red blood cell	RhD	Blood type
none	negative	O negative
none	positive	O positive
A	negative	A negative
A	positive	A positive
B	negative	B negative
B	positive	B positive
A and B	negative	AB negative
A and B	positive	AB positive

20ft (6m)

20/20 vision

If you have 20/20, or normal vision, you can see the letters on an eye test chart clearly from a distance of 20ft (6m).

Hearing frequency range

Animal	Range of hearing frequency in hertz (Hz)
Elephant	below 20
Whale	10–20
Cockroach	100–3,000
Bird	20–15,000
Human	20–20,000
Tiger	10–25,000
Dog	67–45,000
Cat	45–65,000
Bat	2,000–120,000

Calculate your sweat rate

Sweat rate = (A+B) ÷ C

A = body weight before exercise
– body weight after exercise

B = fluid consumed during exercise

C = amount of time
spent exercising

Cold or flu?

Symptom	Cold	Flu
Fever	Sometimes	Above 38°C for 2 days
Headaches	Rare	Common
Muscle aches	Mild	Usual, and often severe
Tiredness/weakness	Mild	Can last 2 or more weeks
Extreme exhaustion	Never	Usual
Stuffy nose/sneezing	Often	Sometimes
Sore throat	Often	Sometimes
Cough	Mild	Usual, and can be severe

Glossary

antibodies
Chemicals, released by white blood cells, that target a specific disease-causing organism and mark it for destruction.

artery
A blood vessel that carries blood away from the heart.

bacteria
A group of single-celled organisms, some of which cause disease.

bases
Four substances – adenine, cytosine, guanine and thymine – that combine to give instructions in molecules of DNA.

bone marrow
Tissue inside bones. Some of it produces new red and white blood cells.

carbohydrate
One of the main components of food. It is broken down in the body to provide energy, partly in the form of glucose.

cell
The basic unit of all living things. A cell is capable of reproducing itself exactly.

DNA (deoxyribonucleic acid)
Molecules that carry the genetic material of living organisms.

enzyme
A substance produced by the body that helps to speed up the rate of chemical reactions in the body.

frequency
The number of sound waves to pass a point in one second. Frequency is measured in units called hertz (Hz).

gene
One of about 20,000 instructions for making and running the human body. Genes are found in DNA molecules.

lymphatic vessels
A network of vessels that carries white blood cells in fluid, called lymph, to the organs of the body's defence system.

microbes
Tiny living things visible only under a microscope. Microbes include bacteria, viruses, fungi, protozoa and algae.

molecule
A chemical unit composed of two or more linked particles called atoms.

neurons
Nerve cells that carry electrical signals through the nervous system.

nucleus
A cell's control centre. It contains DNA.

nutrient
A substance, such as a carbohydrate, vitamin or protein, needed by your body to work properly and keep you alive. You get nutrients from your food and drink.

organ
A part of the body composed of a collection of tissues. Organs are responsible for a particular function. The heart, lungs, liver and spleen are examples of organs in your body.

organelle
One of a number of tiny structures in a cell. Each one has a specific job to do.

plasma
The liquid part of blood. Plasma contains many dissolved substances.

platelets
Disc-shaped cells that are present in large numbers in the blood. They help the blood to clot and form scabs.

protein
A molecule that supplies amino acids to the body and which forms the basis of other substances, such as antibodies.

reflex
An automatic and immediate response by the body. Reflex actions usually protect the body from danger or injury.

REM (rapid eye movement) sleep
The stage of sleep during which the eyeballs are constantly moving.

saliva
A watery fluid, released by glands in the mouth, that helps you to chew, taste and digest your food.

sweat rate
The amount of fluid you lose during each hour of exercise under your normal exercise conditions.

tissue
A group of one type (or similar types) of cells, which work together to perform a particular function. Tissues combine to form an organ.

vein
A vessel that carries blood to the heart.

virus
A microscopic organism that infects and destroys body cells so that it may reproduce itself.

vitamins
A group of substances in food that are vital in tiny amounts for healthy growth.

zygote
The cell produced when an egg is fertilized by the sperm.

Index

63

Find out more

 Books to read

Everything You Need to Know about the Human Body by Patricia Macnair (Kingfisher, 2011)
Human Body Factory by Dan Green (Kingfisher, 2012)
Inside the Human Body by Steve Parker (Miles Kelly, 2012)
The Usborne Complete Book of the Human Body by Anna Claybourne (Usborne, 2006)
Wow! Human Body by Richard Walker (DK, 2012)

 Websites to visit

Click on this website to discover amazing facts about your skeleton:
www.childrensuniversity.manchester.ac.uk/interactives/science/bodyandmedicine/theskeleton

Look closely at blood:
www.e-learningforkids.org/Courses/Liquid_Animation/Body_Parts/Blood/index.html

Watch this film to see how the digestive system works:
http://kidshealth.org/kid/htbw/DSmovie.html

Find out how your body's defence system acts like a castle:
www.cyh.com/HealthTopics/HealthTopicDetailsKids.aspx?p=335&np=152&id=2402

 Places to visit

Discover more about genes and DNA at the 'Who am I?' gallery at:
Science Museum, Exhibition Road, London, SW7 2DD, UK
Telephone: +44 (0) 870 870 4868
www.sciencemuseum.org.uk

Visit At-Bristol and delve into the secrets of the body at the 'All About Us' experience:
At-Bristol, Anchor Road, Harbourside, Bristol, BS1 5DB, UK
Telephone: +44 (0) 845 345 1235
www.at-Bristol.org.uk

Follow the senses at the:
Glasgow Science Centre, 50 Pacific Quay, Glasgow, G51 1EA, UK
Telephone: +44 (0) 141 420 5000
www.gsc.org.uk